IMPROVING FERTILITY IN 30 DAYS

Clearing Fallopian Tubes and a Healthy Pregnancy - The Essential Plan

By Robert Redfern

About The Author

Robert Redfern – Your Personal Health Coach

Robert Redfern (born January 1946) has helped hundreds of thousands of people in over 24 countries through online health support websites, books, radio/TV interviews, and his nutritional discoveries. His new series of books brings this work together in an easy-to-read format that everyone can follow to help resolve their chronic health problem – once and for all.

Robert's interest in health started when he and his wife Anne decided to take charge of their family's health in the late 1980s. Up until 1986, Robert had not taken much notice of his health – in spite of Anne's loving persuasion. It took the premature death of his parents, Alfred and Marjorie, who died in their sixties, to shock Robert into evaluating his priorities.

Robert and Anne looked at the whole field of health, available treatments and the causes of health problems. They found, from doctors researching the causes of disease, that lifestyle and diet were the most important contributions to health. Robert and Anne changed their lifestyle and diet and, together with the use of **HealthPoint**™ acupressure, the improvement to their health was remarkable.

As well as good health, they feel and look younger and more energetic than all those years ago – before they started their plan. At the time of printing, Robert, aged 68, and Anne have every intention of continuing to be well and looking younger, using their unique understanding of Natural Health.

This book is dedicated to Jacob:

Jacob's Story

It breaks my heart when I hear of the desperation and the huge amount of money couples are forced to spend by the medical system with no guarantee of success. The fertility problems are not confined to women; the sperm count of men has fallen by 30% over a 25 year period.

Our daughter-in-law Sian, who is the mother of Jacob, said she is happy for me to tell her story so it may inspire others to follow her example. Sian, like many of today's females, had decided to leave having babies to later in life but then had many problems with spontaneous miscarriages, which the medical system had no successful solutions for.

Like many women, Sian was getting desperate, and so she started on my plan. It was not an obvious move for her as members of my family do not automatically come to me for help, even though I help many thousands around the world. Sian did ask for my help, and although she went onto the supplement plan, she did not take on board the diet recommendations.

The plan seemed fine, and she became pregnant. Things were okay at first, but then on her first scan, the medics noticed a growth, which they said was probably a fibroid. She increased her iodine drops and started to follow the diet to clear this, but again, she miscarried. She then decided to keep to the plan, and the growth was gone in as little as eight weeks.

Now it was time to get serious, and Sian took my advice, which was that the diet was critical. She stopped all carbohydrates and sugar, as well as alcohol, and kept to the Really Healthy Foods plan in this book. The supplement plan was also tightened up and improved. Sian soon became pregnant again, and she kept to the plan and diet meticulously.

This time everything went like a dream, and Jacob Michael Redfern started his new life. We are all really happy for Sian and our son Nicholas, and we're looking forward to helping more couples start a healthy "new life."

Best wishes to you and your healthy family,

Robert Redfern

ROBERT REDFERN – YOUR PERSONAL HEALTH COACH
Provides step-by-step guidance on:

Infertility:
Fertility Problems Affecting
Men & Women

Using the Science of a Non-Inflammatory Lifestyle
to Achieve Fertility and Conceive a Child

Published by

NATURALLY HEALTHY PUBLICATIONS.

From the Publisher:
This book does not intend to diagnose disease nor provide medical advice. Its intention is solely to inform and educate the reader in changing to and living a healthy lifestyle.

Warning:
Some information may be contrary to the opinion of your medical adviser; however, it is not contrary to the science of good health.

CONTENTS

YOUR ACTION PLAN TO COMMIT TO A NON-INFLAMMATORY LIFESTYLE TO ACHIEVE FERTILITY

	ACTION	DATE
I Committed	To a non-inflammatory lifestyle to achieve fertility	
I Committed	To drinking 6-8 glasses of water a day	
I Committed	To getting out in the sun for 20 minutes a day (except when contraindicated)	
I Read	Robert's Infertility Book	
I Ordered	The necessary supplements to facilitate my plan and my healing	
I Planned	My Daily Menu with ReallyHealthyFoods.com	
I Started	My breathing exercises	
I Started	Massaging the acupressure points	
I Reread	Robert's Infertility Book	
I Reviewed	The necessary supplements to facilitate my plan and my healing	
I Reviewed	My water intake	
I Reviewed	My menu	
I Reviewed	My breathing exercises	
I Reviewed	My life-giving sun exposure (except when contraindicated)	
I Reviewed	Massaging the acupressure points	
I Recommitted	To a non-inflammatory lifestyle to achieve fertility	
I Recommitted	To Robert's Infertility Book	
I Recommitted	To taking the necessary supplements to facilitate a non-inflammatory lifestyle	
I Recommitted	To my water intake	
I Recommitted	To following my menu	
I Recommitted	To doing my breathing exercises	
I Recommitted	To life-giving sun exposure (except when contraindicated)	
I Recommitted	To massaging the acupressure points	

What Is Infertility?

According to the A.D.A.M. (Animated Dissection of Anatomy for Medicine) medical encyclopedia:

Infertility simply means the inability to conceive or get pregnant.

Even with this seemingly straightforward explanation, the definition of infertility can be expanded to cover two types of infertility:

1. **Primary Infertility** - A year of regular sex without protection produces no pregnancy. (For a woman 35 or over, the time frame is a minimum of 6 months.)

2. **Secondary Infertility** - At least one pregnancy in the past with no subsequent pregnancies.

Conception

It sounds easy enough to make a baby. Conception is simply the process of bringing a woman's egg together with a man's sperm. Yet according to recent evidence, this process is getting increasingly difficult.

What Is Needed for Conception to Occur?

Other than sexual intercourse three times per week during the female fertile days (just before, during, and just after ovulation), you need:

The right hormones in the right amounts. Conception cannot occur without luteinizing hormone (LH) and follicle-stimulating hormone (FSH).

When conception doesn't take place, where does the problem of infertility lie? Of those who are infertile:

- One out of three men has a problem.
- One out of three women has a problem
- The remaining one out of three may have a problem with both partners.

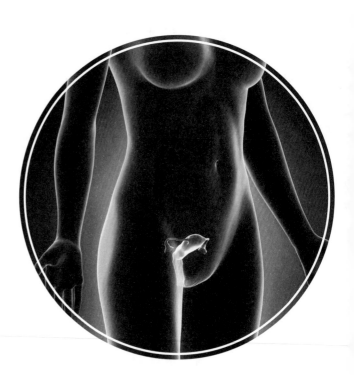

The Modern-Day Epidemic

In Scotland, the sperm count has dropped 30% in 25 years. Even in France, the country famed for its cooking and healthy eating, it has dropped by 25% in just 17 years.

It is heartbreaking for couples who may have left it a little longer than they intended before starting a family (we are at our most fertile by age 20). When they go down the medical route, the money they saved to be able to afford children is spent on dramatically expensive fertility treatments. In most cases, it costs thousands with no guarantee of success.

Of course, doctors never discuss the science and research that shows how diet, sugary drinks, and a lack of nutrients are to blame in the majority of cases. They may then have to admit that it's also the cause of most other diseases. Some of the problems caused by wrong foods and lack of nutrients include the epidemic of infertility, blocked fallopian tubes, cysts, preeclampsia, fibroids, endometriosis, and most gynecological problems.

The facts:

1.   Infertility is an epidemic.
2.   It is breaking many hearts.
3.   It is bankrupting many couples.

Diet, sugary drinks, and lack of essential nutrients are the prime cause. There may be other reasons, but breeders of pedigree dogs and horses know that supplements and the very best diet are essential for healthy offspring.

Nutrition facts and studies show:

- High levels of carbs and other high-sugar foods and drinks increase the risk of fetal damage by over 100%.

- Taking iodine supplements (or having iodine-rich foods in the diet) eliminates the risk of children being born with learning difficulties by 100%.

- Zero level of carbs and high-sugar foods in the diet produces children who do not need glasses.

It is 99% certain that a junk diet and a lack of critical nutrients are to blame for the devastating drop in fertility in women and sperm count in men. Blocked fallopian tubes and scarring are also on the rise. Studies are clear that junk food diets and a lack of critical vitamins and minerals contribute in approximately 50% of all birth defects.

Women and Infertility

A woman with fertility issues may have:

- Irregular periods or amenorrhea (complete absence of menstruation)
- Painful periods
- Two or more miscarriages

Female Fertility Problems

Female infertility can stem from one or a combination of factors:

- Damage to or blockage of the fallopian tube
- Endometriosis
- Inability to ovulate correctly
- Hyperprolactinemia, or elevated levels of prolactin
- Polycystic ovary syndrome (PCOS)

Female infertility is also associated with:

- Early menopause (before 40)
- Uterine fibroids
- Scar tissue (pelvic adhesions)
- Thyroid disorders
- Cancer/cancer treatments
- Hormonal imbalance
- Diabetes and other medical conditions (extreme hyperthyroidism, sickle cell disease, kidney disease)
- Pelvic inflammatory disease (PID)

Men and Infertility

A man with fertility issues may have:

- Inadequate sperm count
- Medical history of testicular, prostate, or sexual dysfunction problems

Male Fertility Problems

Male infertility can stem from one or a combination of factors:

- Too many infections
- Spending too much time in high heat situations, e.g. saunas and hot tubs
- Cancer/cancer treatment
- Impotence
- Hormonal imbalance
- Retrograde ejaculation

Men also need to take care of their prostate gland as this organ is responsible for producing semen.

10 Primary Lifestyle Choices That Affect Fertility

The vast majority of factors affecting fertility stem from lifestyle choices and the inflammation that follows!

The top 10 primary lifestyle choices that affect fertility include choosing to:

1. Have a child later in life

2. Smoke

3. Live under stress

4. Use prescription and/or recreational drugs

5. Have excess body weight

6. Exercise too much

7. Abuse alcohol

8. Use caffeine

9. Expose oneself to environmental toxins

10. Consume a poor diet without supplementing the missing nutrients

1. Having a Child Later in Life

Choosing to have a child later in life can present a problem. Stage of life or age affects fertility primarily in women. As a woman ages, her chances of conceiving a child diminish after she turns 35.

2. Smoking

Study after study after study reveals the link between smoking and infertility for both men and women alike.

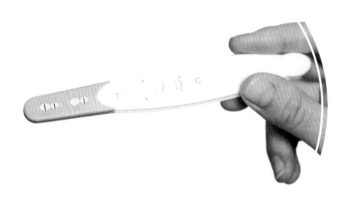

The more cigarettes smoked, the longer the wait to become pregnant.

Female smokers have over a 50% higher rate of delayed conception than females who don't partake in smoking. Secondhand smoke is also a factor.

3. Stress

Stress unfortunately is one of the primary hindrances to good health, as well as fertility in today's society. It may affect as many as 30% of couples who are infertile.

When the body is compromised, several hormones are released that can affect egg production and testosterone levels. Stress may also decrease blood flow to the uterus and diminish the proteins in the lining, which are necessary for the egg to attach.

4. Prescription and/or Recreational Drugs

Infertility caused by taking certain prescription drugs or engaging in the use of recreational drugs may be temporary and cease to exist when the drugs are no longer taken. It is important to address the health concerns the prescription drugs are being prescribed for and to address any addiction problems.

5. Excess Body Weight

Body weight is a considerable factor in the ability to have a baby.

The effects of obesity have been studied and found to be responsible for an over 30% increased risk of:

- Miscarriage
- Irregular periods
- Cesarean sections

What about men? A study composed of over 6,000 men found those who were above a normal, healthy weight had a substantially increased risk of dying from prostate cancer and that "obesity may be a risk factor for fatal prostate cancer." A healthy prostate, not to mention good health in general, is crucial to a man's fertility.

6. Exercising Too Much

The benefits of exercising are well-known. Exercise helps to maintain a healthy body weight and BMI, strengthens the immune system, decreases stress, facilitates a good night's sleep, decreases the risk of chronic disease, and lowers blood pressure.

But you can have too much of a good thing.

Over-exercising can compromise fertility by:

- Decreasing the amount of sperm
- Decreasing estrogen

7. Abusing Alcohol

While an occasional cocktail, beer, or glass of wine is one of life's little pleasures for many of us, imbibing can lower the chances of having a child by:

- Lowering sperm count
- Raising the number of abnormal sperm
- Creating hormonal imbalances
- Leading to zinc malabsorption (zinc is necessary for sperm production)
- Causing irregular menstrual cycles

8. Caffeine

Nutrients are crucial to achieving fertility, and caffeine is a nutrient robber.

Caffeine, due to its stimulating properties, also increases levels of cortisol in the body. Cortisol is the stress hormone, and consistently high levels compromise the adrenal glands. Caffeine can additionally create a hormonal imbalance.

9. Environmental Toxins

One example of the importance of avoiding environmental toxins, specifically pesticides, can be found in a study conducted on men who actually made their living working at a pesticide factory in California.

More than half the workers were diagnosed with azoospermia or oligospermia. Azoospermia, when no detectable sperm can be found in the semen, and oligospermia, a low concentration of sperm in the semen, are both affiliated with very low fertility.

10. Western Un-Natural Food Diet

The "Balanced Western Diet" (now better described as the Western Un-Natural Food Diet) is the number one disease-promoting and inflammation-producing diet in modern society. It is consumed more and more on a daily basis.

This highly inflammatory diet is made up of sugary foods in the form of breads, pastas, cereals, and potatoes. The Western Un-Natural Food Diet is far too high in unhealthy fats and lacks the antioxidants and phytochemicals that are crucial for eliminating free radicals.

For the best results:

- Stop all GMO foods or meats fed on GMO feed—studies show genetically modified foods are a cause of reproductive problems.
- Throw away your weapons of mass destruction—such as the microwave oven.
- Stop all starchy carbs, high-sugar foods, sugar, chemical drinks, and all junk foods.
- Follow the Really Healthy Foods plan in this book.

This typical Western diet is also lacking in high fiber foods and foods that provide the essential nutrients necessary to prevent or control infertility, like:

- Any kind of vegetables - focusing on non-starchy vegetables, especially dark leafy greens. (Yams/sweet potatoes are fine in moderation.)
- Legumes (beans, peas, lentils of all kinds).
- Alternatives to grains and cereals (Quinoa, millet, buckwheat, and other seeds).
- Low-sugar, dark-skinned fruits like avocados, blueberries, blackberries, black currants, etc.
- Hemp seeds daily.

These anti-inflammatory foods will lead to reproductive health in the majority of cases.

Excess Sugar and Your Unborn Baby

Serious diseases caused by excess sugar can start in the womb:

"University of California researchers assessed the diets of 454 mothers of babies born with neural tube defects, like spina bifida. Their diets were compared to the diets of 462 mothers of healthy babies.

The study was published in the American Journal of Clinical Nutrition. For expectant mothers, the results were shocking. The risk of birth defects doubled in pregnant women that ate high-sugar foods, including white rice, white bread, potatoes, and some soft drinks. The risk of birth defects quadrupled in obese women." (Am J Clin Nutr November 2003 vol. 78 no. 5 972-978)

High-sugar foods marketed to children may also be tied to short-sightedness at a young age:

"Diets high in refined starches such as breads and cereals increase insulin levels. This affects the development of the eyeball, making it abnormally long and causing short-sightedness, suggests a team led by Loren Cordain, an evolutionary biologist at Colorado State University in Fort Collins, and Jennie Brand Miller, a nutrition scientist at the University of Sydney.

The theory could help explain the dramatic increase in myopia in developed countries over the past 200 years. It now affects 30 per cent of people of European descent, for example." (Acta Ophthalmologica Scandinavica vol 80, p 125)

What Is Too Much Sugar?

Twelve teaspoons a day may seem generous, but it is very small compared to the 60-70 teaspoons consumed in the average Western diet. 60-70 teaspoons of sugar is UNFIT FOR HUMAN CONSUMPTION.

Sugar in the Western Diet can add up quickly:

- 1 cup of milk = 2 teaspoons of sugar
- 1 bowl of breakfast cereal with milk = 8 teaspoons of sugar
- 1 cup of rice (cooked) = 9 teaspoons of sugar
- 1 banana = 5 teaspoons of sugar
- 1 baked potato (not including skin) = 7 teaspoons of sugar
- 2 slices of bread = 4 teaspoons of sugar
- 1 average soda/soft drink = 8 teaspoons of sugar
- 1 large soda/soft drink = up to 32 teaspoons of sugar

Poison or Moderation?

The unfortunate truth is that the average sugar intake in the modern Western diet is 60 to 70 teaspoons each day. This is causing disease and birth defects—hidden in bad foods, such as breads, cookies, cakes, pasta, parsnips, sodas, fruit juices, breakfast cereals, corn products, white rice, white potatoes, and of course, all processed foods.

If you make it your goal to eat a maximum of 6-12 teaspoons of sugar or 30-60 grams of carbohydrates per day, you will be far ahead of the curve. This sugar must come from fresh, whole foods, outlined in this book.

Diet and Endometriosis

Millions of women suffer from endometriosis, a painful gynecological disorder.

Research has shown women who consume carbs, high-sugar foods, and animal products have a much better chance of fostering the disease than those who eat a healthier diet. The Western Un-Natural Food Diet is also responsible for the hormonal imbalances that help create these problems. Similar findings have linked these diets to fibroids in the uterus and cysts in the ovaries. <u>All three of these conditions are associated with infertility.</u>

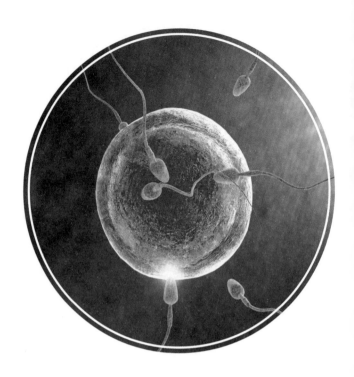

Animals and animal products are now mainly fed on grains, cereals, and other un-natural foods and contaminated with growth hormones, antibiotics, and pesticides.

Links have also been found between serious prostate diseases and a diet of dairy products, eggs, and meat fed on un-natural foods. The conclusions of this and other research suggest that "animal product consumption may be risk factors for poor prostate health."

This confirms that the health of the prostate and thus male fertility are dependent upon eating really healthy foods.

Sources:

1. *Cancer Epidemiol Biomarkers Prev.* 2011 Sep;20(9):1831-7. doi: 10.1158/1055-9965.EPI-11-0402. Epub 2011 Jul 15.

2. M. Inoue-Choi, K. Robien, A. Mariani, J. R. Cerhan, K. E. Anderson. Sugar-Sweetened Beverage Intake and the Risk of Type I and Type II Endometrial Cancer among Postmenopausal Women. Cancer Epidemiology Biomarkers & Prevention, 2013; DOI: 10.1158/1055-9965.EPI-13-0636

3. Radin RG, Palmer JR, Rosenberg L, Kumanyika SK, Wise LA. Dietary glycemic index and load in relation to risk of uterine leiomyomata in the Black Women's Health Study. *Am J Clin Nutr.* 2010;91(5):1281-1288.

4. World Cancer Research Fund/American Institute for Cancer Research. Food, Nutrition, and the Prevention of Cancer: A Global Perspective. *American Institute for Cancer Research*, Washington, D.C., 1997, p. 322.

5. *Cancer Epidemiol Biomarkers Prev.* 2007 Dec;16(12):2623-30.

Fertility Drugs

So what is the usual course of treatment when ovulatory infertility is a problem? Fertility drugs!

These drugs, whether swallowed or injected, are supposedly the answer. Both men and women obviously need to contribute physiologically when it comes to making a baby; however, fertility drugs are only a third as successful when used by men.

Fertility drugs, which are the same for both genders, encourage ovulation and the production of sperm. The FDA has not given the go-ahead for use by men; however, a fertility doctor can recommend them when deemed necessary.

Artificial Insemination

There are several expensive approaches to artificial insemination, with in vitro fertilization (IVF) being the most used. These approaches usually require the use of fertility drugs as well and have a less than 30 % success rate, which decreases after the age of 34.

Infertility and Debt

Maybe it's time for a different approach. Total spend for infertile couples is approaching many billions annually as they try to increase fertility; only a percentage of these couples (up to 35%) are approved for reimbursement.

Can I Reverse Infertility?

Since most cases of infertility are brought on by lifestyle choices, the answer is yes—except in a few rare cases.

Medicine does not offer any cures. (Many people argue that this is on purpose since it would put Big Pharma out of business.) However, everything has a cause. Take away the cause, apply the science of a non-inflammatory lifestyle, and your body will be able to repair itself with a little bit of help. Support tissue regeneration with a healthy lifestyle and the proper nutrients, and in the majority of cases you can become healthy again.

Remember, these conditions are inflammatory in nature and, therefore, will benefit from an anti-inflammatory approach. By hydrating the body {6-8 x 500ml (16oz) glasses a day} with pure, clean water and replenishing it with the proper nutrients and antioxidants in the form of vitamins, minerals, essential fatty acids, healthy carbohydrates, and amino acids, the repair and healing of the body can start to take place.

Nutritional therapy supports healing.

The initial detox can be uncomfortable but only temporarily.

Eating right can minimize the effects.

. . . regenerate with healthy lifestyle and nutrients . . .

Down to Basics

Pregnancy is (or should be) the result of sexual intercourse in a loving relationship. As unromantic as it sounds, it may take a little planning and timing.

Ovulation

There is a just one time in the monthly cycle when a woman is fertile. This falls a few days before, during, and after ovulation. Ovulation occurs when the most mature of the eggs is released into one of the fallopian tubes. To conceive, sperm must reach the mature egg before it dies.

A typical egg can live 12 to 24 hours after ovulation, while sperm can survive up to five days in a healthy vaginal environment.

Therefore, fertile days are the five days preceding ovulation and up to two days after ovulation. This lasts about a week. Strange as it seems, this week can be easily missed, unless you time it just right. By having sexual intercourse three times just before ovulation, the chances of pregnancy dramatically increase in a healthy couple.

Ovulation Testing Kits

If you don't want to chance missing your fertile window, you can take advantage of inexpensive technology. Digital ovulation tests are now available, such as the Clearblue Digital Ovulation Test. A test like this is designed to measure the rise of LH ovulation hormones 24-36 hours before ovulation to determine the best two days to conceive within a cycle.

Timing sexual intercourse within these two days will provide the best odds of conception.

A digital ovulation test can be used to test a woman's urine once a day at the same time each day. When tested during the anticipated time of ovulation in a cycle, an ovulation test kit can provide up to 99% accuracy in detecting LH hormone surges. Manual ovulation tracking or a digital test can identify a woman's monthly fertile window prior to conception.

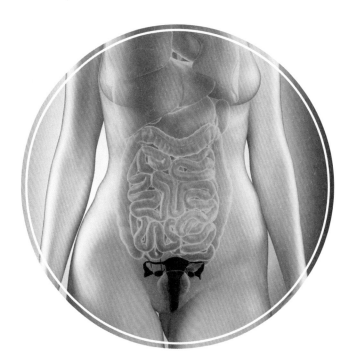

The Nutrients You Need

Studies show the following nutrients will help prevent or control infertility in most people:

Serrapeptase SerraEnzyme with MSM and Trace Minerals - Clears any scarring and inflammation in the reproductive organs, such as the fallopian tubes or testicles. Take 2 x 3 times a day, 30 minutes before eating. Drop to 1 x 3 after one month (plan on four months).

Curcumin - Can relieve any pain and inflammation in the body, in particular the sex organs. Take 1 capsule x 3 times per day.

Nascent Iodine - Supports the thyroid gland and the immune system. Iodine deficiency is thought to be the cause of ovarian cysts and polycystic ovaries. Take 10 drops x 4 times a day in 25ml of water.

BioAstin® Astaxanthin - Powerful antioxidant that can boost and enhance the immune system. It can also aid and improve fertility. Take 2 veg softgels, 2 times per day.

Maca Extract - Balances the endocrine and hormonal system. Take 1-2 teaspoons daily.

90 Sublingual Vitamins and Minerals - Supports the whole body and immune system. Take 15ml or ½ oz., 2 times per day with food.

Vitamin D3 - Supports healthy hormonal balance and the immune system. Take 1 capsule, 1-2 times per day.

Why Doesn't My Doctor Tell Me About This Plan?

The Non-Inflammatory Lifestyle Program can help you get better! Your doctor is obliged to conform to the medical model that is designed to maintain the monopoly that the pharmaceutical industry, the GMC in the UK and the AMA in the USA, have over all things connected with the health of individuals.

These organizations make profits by caring for sick people and do not have a business model that caters to real healthcare and recovery. They pursue a patented drug model where they can charge exorbitant prices for a lifetime of drugs that, at best, help individuals feel better and, at worse, speed up their death.

These industries are not designed to get anyone healthy, ever!

In the USA, they are shielded by the FDA and in the UK by the MHRA. The political parties and the most powerful politicians all receive money from these organizations and are responsible for making the laws that perpetuate this disease management monopoly.

When carefully followed, the Non-Inflammatory Lifestyle Program will show results within 30 days.

The Infertility Rehabilitation Plan
Your 10 Steps to a Healthy Future

The following protocol works for any type of infertility, to some extent.

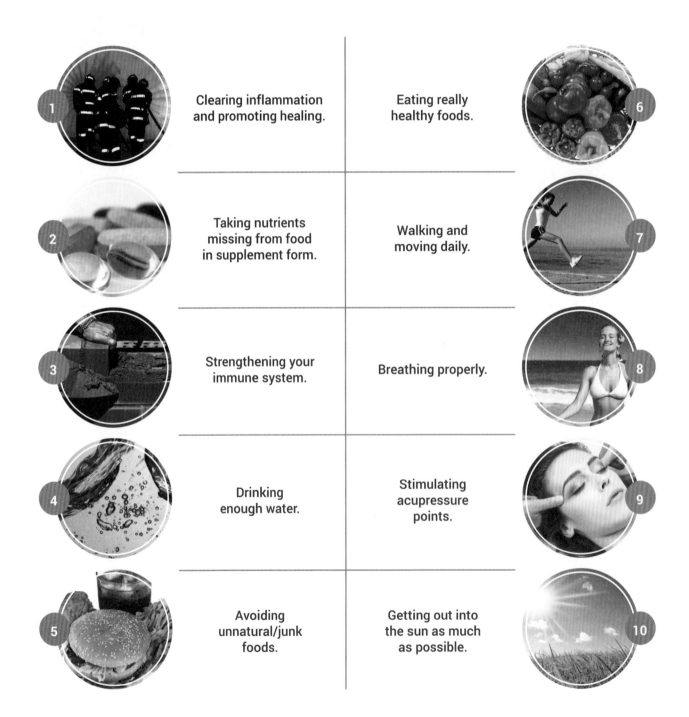

1. Clearing inflammation and promoting healing.

2. Taking nutrients missing from food in supplement form.

3. Strengthening your immune system.

4. Drinking enough water.

5. Avoiding unnatural/junk foods.

6. Eating really healthy foods.

7. Walking and moving daily.

8. Breathing properly.

9. Stimulating acupressure points.

10. Getting out into the sun as much as possible.

It is almost unheard of for a person applying a good percentage of these lifestyle changes to their daily life to not clear their infertility symptoms to some extent, and in many cases completely.

For details of the following suggested formulas, turn to **page 37.**

1. Clearing Inflammation and Promoting Healing

Basic Plan: Clearing Fallopian Tubes

SerraPlus+ 80,000IU - **Clears any scarring and inflammation in the reproductive organs. Take 2 x 3 times a day, 30 minutes before eating. Drop to 1 x 3 after one month (plan on four months).**

Curcuminx4000 - **Contains Meriva® (root) Curcuma longa extract; relieves pain and inflammation in the body. Take 1 capsule x 3 times per day.**

Nascent Iodine Drops - **Contains Iodine in its atomic form; regulates metabolism and supports the thyroid gland. Take 4 x 4 drops per day in 25ml of water, swish around the mouth for 30 seconds before swallowing. Build over 2 weeks to 10 x 4 until well and then slowly reduce back to 4 x 4.**

2. Taking the Missing Nutrients

Advanced Fertility Plan

SerraPlus+ 80,000IU - **Contains Serrapeptase SerraEnzyme. Clears any scarring and inflammation in the reproductive organs. Take 2 x 3 times a day, 30 minutes before eating. Drop to 1 x 3 after one month (plan on four months).**

Curcuminx4000 - **Contains Meriva® (root) Curcuma longa extract; relieves pain and inflammation in the body. Take 1 capsule x 3 times per day.**

Nascent Iodine Drops - **Contains Iodine in its atomic form; regulates metabolism and supports the thyroid gland. Take 4 x 4 drops per day in 25ml of water, swish around the mouth for 30 seconds before swallowing. Build over 2 weeks to 10 x 4 until well and then slowly reduce back to 4 x 4.**

Astaxanthin - **Enhances the immune system and supports fertility. Take 2 veg softgels, 2 times per day.**

MacaPro - **Balances the endocrine and hormonal system. Take 1-2 teaspoons daily.**

3. Immune Recovery and Strengthening

Ultimate Fertility Plan

SerraPlus+ 80,000IU - **Contains Serrapeptase SerraEnzyme. Clears any scarring and inflammation in the reproductive organs. Take 2 x 3 times a day, 30 minutes before eating. Drop to 1 x 3 after one month (plan on four months).**

Curcuminx4000 - **Contains Meriva® (root) Curcuma longa extract; relieves pain and inflammation in the body. Take 1 capsule x 3 times per day.**

Nascent Iodine Drops - **Contains Iodine in its atomic form; regulates metabolism and supports the thyroid gland. Take 4 x 4 drops per day in 25ml of water, swish around the mouth for 30 seconds before swallowing. Build over 2 weeks to 10 x 4 until well and then slowly reduce back to 4 x 4.**

Astaxanthin - **Enhances the immune system and supports fertility. Take 2 veg softgels, 2 times per day.**

MacaPro - **Balances the endocrine and hormonal system. Take 1-2 teaspoons daily.**

Active Life - **Contains a full spectrum of 90 vitamins and minerals. Take 15ml or ½ oz., 2 times per day with food.**

Vitamin D3 - **Contributes to hormonal balance. Take 1 capsule, 1-2 times per day.**

Recommended Nutrients - but Suggested for the First 1 to 2 Months At Least

UB8Q10 Ubiquinol - Supports strong sperm in males (in studies). Take 1 capsule, 2 times daily. If over 35 years old, take 2 softgel capsules x 2 times per day.

Rosavin - Reduces stress and balances emotions in both men and women. Take 1 capsule, 2 times a day.

While this book is designed to improve fertility in women, a sample male fertility plan can be found below:

MALE FERTILITY - STRONGER SPERM AND EJACULATION HEALTH PLAN

The health plan below is designed to improve sperm count and male fertility. By following the supplement regimen and choosing a naturally healthy lifestyle in the long term, it's possible to boost your fertility and overall health.

Your 4-8 Week Plan, From My eBook, by Robert Redfern

Supplements to support men's fertility - in order of priority:

UB8Q10 Ubiquinol - Essential for stronger sperm. Eight times more effective at restoring cell energy than CoQ10. Take 2 capsules x 2 times a day with food.

Prostate Plus+™ - Aids in healthy sperm flow. Take 2-4 capsules per day.

Nascent Iodine Drops - Regulates the metabolism and supports the thyroid gland. Take 4 drops x 4 times a day in 25ml of water, swish around the mouth for 30 seconds before swallowing. Build over 2 weeks to 10 x 4 until well and then slowly reduce back to 4 x 4. Note that Iodine needs a supplement containing selenium to activate it such as ActiveLife 90 or Daily Immune Protection.

Astaxanthin - A powerful antioxidant that boosts and enhances the reproductive system. Take 2 x 2 times per day.

MacaPro - Balances the hormonal system. Take 1-2 teaspoons daily.

ActiveLife 90 - A full spectrum of 90 vitamins and minerals. Take 15ml or 1/2 oz. 2 times per day with food.

B4 Health Spray - Contributes to hormonal balance. Take 4 sprays, 1-2 times per day.

4. Drink More Water.

Drink 6-8 glasses of distilled or RO filtered water per day, with a large pinch of bicarbonate of soda (baking soda) for internal organ support.

5. Cut Out Unnatural Foods.

Until pregnant and a healthy baby is finished breastfeeding, stop eating all starchy carbohydrates (breads, pastry, cookies, breakfast cereals, potatoes, and pasta), processed foods, and cow's milk products.

Note: Do not eat potatoes, parsnips, turnips, and rice (except for a small amount of wild or brown rice and yams/sweet potatoes).

6. Eat Really Healthy Foods.

Make sure to eat some of these foods every two hours for the first few months of recovery:

Eat 9-14 portions of fresh or frozen veggies daily (in soups, juiced, stir-fried, steamed, etc.); 50% raw juiced (use the pulp in soups) and organic if possible. Blended makes for better digestion.

Eat 5 portions of antioxidant-rich, dark-skinned fruits (blueberries, cherries, red grapes, etc.) daily.

Avocados are the all-time superfood with nearly a full spectrum of nutrients. If they are available where you live, make sure you have at least 2 per day for good health recovery. All senile dementia issues (as well as cancer and heart disease) are helped by these.

Eat 5 portions of beans, nuts, and seeds (soaked and mashed for the nuts and seeds).

If you want to eat meat, then choose pasture-fed meats or chicken and eat only a small amount weekly. Grass-fed is healthier than grain or corn-fed animals.

If you eat fish, then eat at least 3-4 portions per week of oily fish and vary it by choosing fish such as salmon, sardines, mackerel, etc. Even canned fish is very nutritious, and wild caught fish is best.

Include Hemp, Omega 3, or Krill oil and other healthy oils like Olive oil and Coconut oil.

As healthy alternatives to carbs, consider Quinoa, Chia Seeds, Amaranth, Buckwheat, and Millet Seeds. Cous Cous can be used, except for those who are allergic to gluten proteins (celiacs, etc.).

Take 3-5 (depending upon your body mass and the heat) teaspoons of Sea or Rock Salt daily in food or a little water. Sea or Rock Salt does not contain the critical mineral iodine, so add Nascent Iodine to your daily dose.

Which vegetables to eat

Note: Not all fruits listed are available in every country.

- Artichoke
- Asian Vegetables Sprouts (Wheat, Barley, Alfalfa, etc)
- Asparagus
- Avocado
- Broad Beans
- Cabbage (various types)
- Dandelion Leaves
- Dried Peas
- Fennel
- Garden Peas
- Garlic
- Kale
- Lettuce (Kos and various types)
- Mangetout Peas
- Mushrooms
- Petit Pois Peas
- Runner Beans
- Seaweed all types (Kelp, Wakame, Noni, etc)

- Sugar Snap Peas
- Beetroot
- Broccoli
- Brussel Sprouts
- Capsicum
- Carrots
- Cauliflower
- Celeriac
- Choko
- Cucumber
- Eggplant (Aubergine) Kale
- Kohlrabi
- Kumara
- Okra
- Onions (Red and White)
- Radishes
- Silver Beet
- Spinach
- Squash
- Zucchini (Courgettes)

Which fruits to eat

Note: Not all fruits listed are available in every country.

- Apple
- Apricot
- Avocado
- Blackberries
- Blackcurrants
- Bilberries
- Blueberries
- Cherries
- Cherimoya
- Dates
- Damsons
- Durian
- Figs
- Gooseberries
- Grapes
- Grapefruit
- Kiwi fruit

- Limes
- Lychees
- Mango
- Nectarine
- Orange
- Pear
- Plum/Prune (dried Plum)
- Pineapple
- Pomegranate
- Raspberries
- Western raspberry (blackcap)
- Rambutan
- Salal berry
- Satsuma
- Strawberries
- Tangerine

The Garden of Eden Pyramid

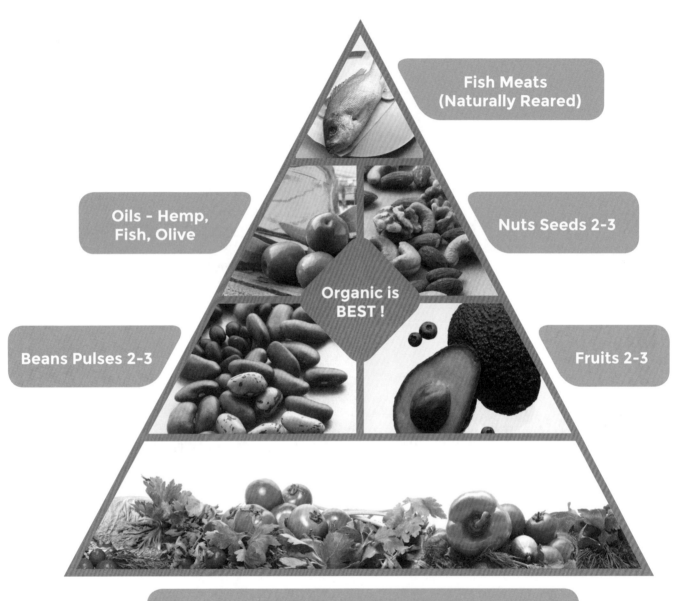

Fish Meats (Naturally Reared)

Oils - Hemp, Fish, Olive

Nuts Seeds 2-3

Organic is BEST !

Beans Pulses 2-3

Fruits 2-3

Vegetables (not root): 8-12 portions per day
At least 1/2 should be raw, as in salad, etc.

Movement is a vital part of your recovery plan.

7. Walking and Moving Daily

Contrary to the opinion of fitness fanatics, there are simple ways to get your body working healthier and stronger. You can also include swimming, if desired.

One of the two simple ways to exercise is to build up to walking 3-5 miles per day, in a fast, purposely strong way with as long a stride as you can. Keep your hands moving from chest level to belt level as you move with each stride.

If this is difficult for you at the start, and your lungs are weak, then lie down to exercise to make it easier.

Hold your head high.

Focus your eyes 15 feet to 20 feet in front of you.

Keep your chin parallel to the ground.

Move shoulders naturally and freely.

Gently tighten stomach muscles.

Tuck your pelvis under your torso.

Swing your arms in a natural motion while walking briskly.

Position your feet parallel to each other, if comfortable, and shoulder-width apart.

Lie down in a comfortable place. On your bed (if it's firm enough), when you first wake up is a great time and place for this. Bring a knee up to your chest as high as you can get it and then alternate with the other knee. Do as many of these as you can while keeping count. Do this every day and set yourself targets to increase the speed and the number as the weeks go by. You should be doing enough to make your lungs and heart beat faster. At the same time, as you improve your count on your back you need to be starting your walking and building this up.

8. Learn Proper Breathing.

It is critical to breathe properly for a healthy body. Oxygen is the prime source of health.

There are two ways to breathe:

1. **Anxious Breathing: In the chest.**
2. **Relaxed Breathing: In the diaphragm or stomach area.**

The first breath in the chest is part of the stress response and involves hormones such as cortisol. This type of breathing should last no longer than it takes to deal with a problem in life and then another hormone kicks in to create relaxed breathing. If this stress type of breathing becomes chronic or habitual, then the cortisol and retained carbon dioxide become part of the problem, and the body's natural healthy systems cannot function properly. It also weakens the immune system and opens you up to infections.

Your goal is to relearn relaxed, healthy breathing, where you clear cortisol and carbon dioxide. Too much carbon dioxide in your bloodstream destroys something called hemoglobin, which is the blood's method of carrying oxygen around the body. So it's critical to be able to breathe in a relaxed way from the diaphragm.

HOW TO BREATHE PROPERLY

The simple way to learn is to lie on your back in a firm bed or on the floor on a blanket or mat. Put a bit of weight over your belly button, such as a heavy book. Take a breath into your nose so that the book rises as you fill your diaphragm (tummy) with air. Hold the breath in your tummy for the count of 4 and then breathe out through your nose and feel your tummy deflating. Let go of any tension you may have with the out-breath. Then repeat. Your upper chest should not move at all, which shows you are relaxed and not stress breathing.

Practice over and again while lying down, and once you have really got the long, slow rhythm of relaxed breathing, then try it standing up. You may feel dizzy to begin with getting all this fresh oxygen, but you must practice this every spare minute you have.

9. Stimulate Acupressure Points.

Another part of your fertility plan is to stimulate acupressure points connected to the reproductive system. There are various points that you can massage gently with your finger or stimulate with an electronic stimulator that mimics the action of acupuncture. The recommended device is **HealthPoint™**, and you can read more about this on **page 41.**

10. Getting Out into the Sun As Much As Possible

A critical vitamin for a healthy body is Vitamin D3. There is a large dose of this in the important supplement I recommend on **page 39**, but it is still important to still get some Vitamin D from the sun.

The sun is the bringer of all life, and a silly myth has developed that the sun is our enemy and we should keep out of it, or worse still, put some toxic chemicals all over us so we can go out in it.

I am not saying that we can go out on a really hot sunny day and lie in the sun for 6 hours for the first time. We are supposed to build the skin's tolerance to the sun over many weeks in the spring to stimulate protection from it, so that by the time the hot summer sun comes along we can tolerate much more.

Recommendations for sun exposure:

A: Expose as much skin as you can to the sun each day, such as on your morning walk.

B: Build up your sun exposure gradually from spring to summer seasons.

C: Try to stay out of the sun in midday without a cover-up; a cover-up is preferred to sunscreen.

D: If you do use sunscreen or sun cream, purchase organic products instead of chemical-based, name-brand creams.

E: It's important to remember that the sun is your friend and sunshine can be enjoyed in moderation!

More About Clearing Inflammation and Promoting Healing

SerraPlus+™ 80,000IU Capsules

SerraPlus+™ with pure MSM is the Serrapeptase enzyme that helps to prevent and remove dead tissue and unhealthy inflammation, allowing the body's naturally healthy processes to function. Taking Serrapeptase can clear scarring and inflammation in the reproductive organs.

Ingredients:

*   Serrapeptase - 80,000 IU

*   Trace Minerals - 50 mg

*   MSM (Methylsulfonylmethane) - 350 mg

Dosage:

Take 2 x 3 times a day, 30 minutes before eating. Drop to 1 x 3 after one month (plan on four months).

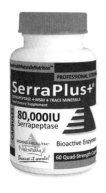

Curcumin

Curcumin (from Turmeric) has been used for thousands of years for its antibacterial, anti-viral, anti-inflammatory, and anti-fungal properties. Curcumin's disease fighting potential has been studied and demonstrated against several types of cancer, diseases of the vascular system, type II diabetes, atopic dermatitis, arthritis, psoriasis, and Crohn's disease, among others.

Due to its inherent poor absorbency, high doses of ordinary Curcumin95% have been needed to achieve the dramatic effects show in worldwide studies. Now CurcuminX4000™ resolves this with its unique high utilization formulation.

Ingredients:

*   Meriva® (root) Curcuma longa extract – 600mg

Dosage:

Take 1 capsule x 3 times per day.

Nascent Iodine Colloidal Drops

Nascent Iodine is totally different from the typical iodine in its denser state sold as an antiseptic, or as iodine tri-chloride (claiming to be atomized), or as added to potassium iodide to make it soluble in liquid. Nascent Iodine is consumable iodine in its atomic form rather than its molecular form. It can provide benefits in thyroid and immune support, detoxification, metabolism, improved energy, and more.

Ingredients:

*   Iodine (in its atomic form) - 400 µg

Dosage:

Take 4 drops x 4 times a day in 25ml of water.

More About Missing Nutrients

Astaxanthin

Astaxanthin is a powerful antioxidant that boosts and enhances the immune system. Studies have shown that this new antioxidant exhibits strong free radical scavenging activities and protects against lipid peroxidation and oxidative damage of LDL-cholesterol, cell membranes, cells, and tissues. It may prevent damage to the retina caused by strong sunlight.

Ingredients:

- Vitamin A (as Beta Carotene) – 195IU
- Vitamin E (d-alpha tocopherol) – 30IU
- BioAstin® Natural Astaxanthin – 12mg
- Lutein – 120mcg

Dosage:

Take 2 capsules, 2 times a day.

MacaPro

MacaPro balances the endocrine and hormonal system. Maca is a plant that grows only on the high Junin Plateau in Peru and has been highly esteemed for its unique nutritional value for over 2000 years.

Maca is not a drug or a vitamin, it is a food source that is very high in polypeptides (building blocks of proteins), amino acids, and fatty acids—together with an impressive array of bioactive compounds, any or all of which may be responsible for its remarkable benefits.

Ingredients:

- Maca Extract - 1140mg

Dosage:

Take 1-2 teaspoons daily.

More About Immune Strengthening Formulations

Active Life 90

Active Life 90 Powerful Liquid Vitamins & Minerals is a liquid formula to ensure you get all the essential vitamins and minerals needed by your body. This single liquid supplement allows for maximum absorption and utilization of the body - 300% more absorbent than tablets!

Ingredients: / Amount per Serving

Ingredients:	Amount per Serving
Calories	39
Calcium (Tricalcium Phosphate, Citrate)	600mg
Choline Bitartrate	25mg
Chromium (Chromium Polynicotinate)	200mcg
Copper (Copper Gluconate)	2mg
Folic Acid (Vitamin B Conjugate)	500mcg
Inositol	50mg
Magnesium (Citrate Gluconate Concentrate)	300mg
Manganese (Manganese Gluconate)	10mg
Organic Seleniumethionine	200mcg
Potassium (Potassium Gluconate)	250mg
Vitamin A (Palmitate)	5000IU
Vitamin A (Beta Carotene)	5000IU
Vitamin B1 (Thiamine Mononitrate)	3mg
Vitamin B12 (Methylcobalamin)	6mcg
Vitamin B2 (Riboflavin)	3.4mg
Vitamin B3 (Niacinamide)	40mg
Vitamin B5 (Calcium Pantothenate)	20mg
Vitamin B6 (Pyridoxine Hydrochloride)	4mg
Vitamin C (Ascorbic Acid)	300mg
Vitamin D (Cholecalciferol)	400IU
Vitamin E (Alpha Tocopheryl Acetate)	60IU
Vitamin K (Phytonadione)	80mcg
Zinc (Oxide)	15mg
Ionic Trace Minerals	600mg
Phosphorus (Amino Acid Chelate)	190mg
Biotin	300mcg
Iodine (Potassium Iodine)	150mcg
Boron (Sodium Borate)	2mg
Molybdenum	75mcg
Chloride Concentrate	102mg
Amino Acid Complex	10mg
Aloe Vera Extract (200:1)	2mg

Dosage:

Take ½ oz. (15ml) with breakfast and ½ oz. with evening meal. Mix with juice or water.

Vitamin D3

Vitamin D is a precursor hormone—the building block of a powerful steroid hormone in your body called calcitriol. As a hormone, calcitriol controls phosphorus, calcium, and bone metabolism and neuromuscular function in the body. For centuries, Vitamin D was considered to be only essential to maintaining bone health, but recently, more and more studies are linking Vitamin D to overall body wellness and hormonal balance.

Ingredients:

*   Vitamin D3 (Natural Cholecalciferol) – 5000IU
*   Calcium (Natural Calcium Carbonate) – 100mg

Dosage:

Take 1 capsule, 1-2 times per day.

Recommended Nutrients - but Suggested for the First 1 to 2 Months At Least

UB8Q10 Ubiquinol

CoQ10 or coenzyme Q10 is a greatly beneficial vitamin-like enzyme that is present in almost all plant, animal, and human cells. Coenzyme Q10 is considered as your body's POWERHOUSE ENHANCER and ANTIOXIDANT. UB8Q10, also known as Ubiquinol, is a Coenzyme Q10 that is 8 times better absorbed compared to ordinary Coq10! UB8Q10 supports strong sperm in males, according to studies.

Ingredients:

*   Ubiquinol CoQH* - 100mg

Dosage:

Take 1 capsule, 2 times daily. If over 35 years old, take 2 softgel capsules x 2 times per day.

Rosavin

Siberian Rhodiola Rosea provides an adaptogenic response to a number of environmental stressors. It helps to fight mood swings, enhance memory and mental performance, assist in maintaining energy levels and stamina, increase circulation in the brain, and aid weightin both men and women.

Ingredients:

*   Proprietary Blend – 100mg
*   (Standardized 3% Siberian Rhodiola Rosea) bioactive Rosavin, Rosin, Rosarin, and Salidroside

Dosage:

Take 1 capsule, 2 times a day.

More About Acupressure

Stimulating the points in page 8.26 of the book Mastering Acupuncture will help to balance the reproductive system. These points can be effectively and safely stimulated using the **HealthPoint™** electro-acupressure kit. The advantage of the kit is it gives you the power to precisely locate the acupuncture point, and indeed other points, so you can enjoy the benefits of acupuncture at home and without any needles.

HealthPoint™ is easy to use, painless, and effective. It includes an instructional DVD and book covering over 150 pain and non-pain conditions that can be helped, such as headaches, back, neck, and joint problems.

The gentle and systematic stimulation of the body's natural healing system can speed recovery in many cases. **HealthPoint™** breakthrough technology was developed with leading pain control specialist Dr. Julian Kenyon MD 21 years ago, and today features the latest microchip technology to quickly locate acupuncture points key to specific health conditions, such as the points for infertility.

In Conclusion:

The Non-Inflammatory Lifestyle Program is a complete program, one designed to address all aspects of what is required to prevent or control your infertility.

Infertility is essentially a lifestyle disease, meaning if the lifestyle is changed, there is every likelihood of some recovery. With the changes in this 10 Step Plan put into effect, the body is perfectly capable of healing and recovering good health.

Drugs won't improve your health.

Drugs do not work in that they do not make you healthy. At best, drugs will help you feel better; at worst, they will speed up degeneration and contribute to premature death.

The pharmaceutical business would prefer you continue your present, ineffective treatment plan, only utilizing toxic pills in the form of immune-suppressing drugs and avoiding the true path to prevention and healing.

You are now learning there is a better way.

The Non-Inflammatory Lifestyle Program is structured for those patients struggling to prevent or control their infertility, even after other medical treatments have failed

- A program that can help you learn how to love your health and improve your quality of life through treatment in the form of exercise, education, and coaching.

- A personalized program that incorporates therapy and support, assisting the person in achieving the maximum results possible.

The Non-Inflammatory Lifestyle Program is detailed within this book and, when carefully followed, will show results within weeks.

You will always end up healthier with this plan.

The worst thing that can happen with this plan is that you will get healthier but still need to take drugs if they or the disease have damaged you to the extent that you are reliant on them.

Take it all slowly and step by step.

Unless you are already used to making changes in your life, you will find adopting these habits of healthy living can be difficult to sustain. Persist. Because...

Make no mistake... Your life is worth it.

Robert Redfern, Your Health Coach

Email Robert@goodhealth.nu
www.MyGoodHealthClub.com
for step by step coaching and support.

Sample Daily Fertility Rehabilitation Plan

TIME	ACTION	AMOUNT
OPTIONAL ITEMS		
Just before eating	UB8Q10 Ubiquinol	Take 1 capsule, 2 times per day. If over the age of 35, take 2 x 2 times per day
Just before eating	Rosavin	Take 1 capsule, 2 times a day
BREAKFAST		
30 minutes before breakfast	SerraPlus+ 80,000IU	2 capsules, with water
Just before eating	Curcuminx4000™	Take 1 capsule
Just before eating	Nascent Iodine Colloidal Drops	Take 4 drops in 25ml of water
With breakfast	MacaPro®	1 teaspoon
Any time after breakfast	AstaXanthin™	Take 2 capsules
Any time after breakfast	Nascent Iodine Drops	4 drops in 25ml of water
BREAK		
BEFORE A BREAK	Nascent Iodine Colloidal Drops	Take 4 drops in 25ml of water
LUNCH		
30 minutes before lunch	SerraPlus+ 80,000IU	Take 2 capsules, with water
Just before eating	Curcuminx4000™	1 capsule
Just before eating	Nascent Iodine Colloidal Drops	Take 4 drops in 25ml of water
With lunch	AstaXanthin™	Take 2 capsules
With lunch	ActiveLife™	Take 15ml
With lunch	Vitamin D3	Take 1 capsule
EVENING MEAL		
30 minutes before evening meal	SerraPlus+ 80,000IU	Take 2 capsules, with water
Just before eating	Nascent Iodine Colloidal Drops	Take 4 drops in 25ml of water
Just before eating	Curcuminx4000™	Take 1 capsule
With the evening meal	Active Life™	Take 15ml or ½ floz. in juice or water
With the evening meal	MacaPro®	Take 1 teaspoon
With the evening meal	Vitamin D3	Take 1 capsule

All the books in this series:

Uterine Fibroids

Endometriosis

Menopause

Healthy Pregnancy

Polycystic Ovarian Syndrome

Osteoporosis

Other Books by Robert Redfern:

The 'Miracle Enzyme' is Serrapeptase

Turning A Blind Eye

Mastering Acupuncture

EquiHealth Equine Acupressure